SHERRINGHAMIA

The Journal of Abbot Upcher

1813 - 16

✳ ✳ ✳

Edited by Susan Yaxley

GW00459159

The Larks Press
Stibbard, Norfolk

*First edition of 400 copies printed and published by
the Larks Press
Ordnance Farm House, Guist Bottom, Dereham, Norfolk
November 1986*

*First reprint July 1987
Second reprint July 1992*

*The editor wishes to thank the H. T. S. Upcher Trust for
permission to publish this journal.*

ISBN 0 948400 04 8

An Introduction to the Upchers of Sheringham

Abbot Upcher, the author of this brief journal, was born in 1784, the third son of Peter and Elizabeth Upcher of Ormesby, Norfolk. His two elder brothers died tragically in their teens, one as a result of a riding accident, the other from smallpox. After his father's death in 1796, therefore, Abbot, the only surviving son, became a young man of independent means.

At a 'public breakfast and morning dance' in Yarmouth in 1808 Abbot Upcher met Charlotte Wilson, the eighteen-year-old daughter of the Reverend Henry Wilson of Kirby Cane who was later to inherit the title of Baron Berners. A brief courtship followed and the couple were married on April 3rd 1809. The sun shone, we are told, but there was snow on the ground.

After their marriage the young Upchers leased a house at Thompson, near Watton, but also stayed frequently in Yarmouth and Kirby Cane. They shared a keen interest in literature and a strong sense of religion. Abbot read daily from the Bible or from volumes of sermons, but he also loved the sport of coursing and Charlotte was interested in botany.

Their first son, Henry Ramey Upcher, was born on

March 8th 1810. Childbirth evidently came easily to Charlotte and a daughter, Charlotte Mary, followed a year later. Abbot began to search for a suitable country seat for his growing family. After failing to obtain first an estate at Wroxham, and then Mount Ida at Bagthorpe, he finally settled on Sheringham. Although he was disappointed in the house, 'it being only a better kind of farm house', he was carried away by the 'beautiful and romantic grounds', and on July 10th 1811 he signed the agreement with Mr Cook Flower to purchase the property.

Flower's agent for this sale was William Repton of Aylsham, and his father, Humphry Repton, the great landscape gardener, was quickly engaged to design a new mansion for the Upchers. He prepared one of his celebrated 'Red Books' for Sheringham and this still survives. He later described Sheringham Bower as his 'favourite and darling child in Norfolk'.

Abbot Upcher set about building his new house and laying out the park with energy and enthusiasm. He adored his wife and delighted in his children who were eventually to number three sons and three daughters. A future of great happiness seemed to lie before them. 'What infinite variety' he wrote, 'presents itself in this enchanting spot ...... Oh! what scenes of rational yet heartfelt pleasure do we not anticipate in the lovely Sheringham'.

SHERRINGHAMIA

❀   ❀   ❀

Commenc'd at Sherringham Decr. 19th 1813

I have often thought how interesting it would be to read those little transactions, those little events in which our Ancestors have been more immediately engaged, that one might not merely know their names, but also be made acquainted with their sentiments and benefitted by their experience, were their opinions committed to writing. What an interesting work surely it would have been to their descendants had each succeeding head of a family contributed the Volume of his life, or even the account of the improvements of his Estate. The latter of these is the object of the following pages.

Wednesday July 10th 1811, half past 6 or 7 p.m.

I signed the agreement for Sherringham, for which I gave £52,500.

Sherringham was bought with a part of the money derived from the sale of my scatter'd farms in Suffolk and Essex.

June 10th 1812 Wednesday.

Repton met Charlotte and myself at Sherringham, to fix the site and approach to the New House, but without success tho' employed about it several hours.

June 11th 1812, Thursday

Repton decided on the spot and the approach, for which I shall never cease to thank him, and those who come after me, conscious of the blessing of being screened from the snowy north, will learn perhaps to thank him also — and will they hallow the memory of Abbot Upcher whose pride it is to have been the Founder of his Family at Sherringham?

13th October, 1812

Came to take possession of Sherringham and slept at Pauls farm. Flower's things were not completely out of the House till the 15th. On the 16th of Octr. we first dined in our own house.

18th Octr.

Left Sherringham for Yarmouth, where I staid till the 22nd when I went to Bury to see Sparke, my Sollicitor on the sale of my Suffolk Farms. Return'd to my beloved Wife, dear to me beyond measure, on the 24th when I was seiz'd with a violent nervous fever. Dr. Girdlestone attended, from whom I deriv'd no benefit whatsoever. On the 28th Providence kindly sent to me my most esteem'd, most faithfull friend and schoolfellow, the Rev'd John Wilkinson, who attended me, with my dear Wife, to London, where I immediately became the patient of that friendly, humane man (& relative by marriage) Dr. Heberden. After being under his constant and affectionate attendance till the 17th of December. I left London on the 18th, our faithful & providential friend Wilkinson (Henry Ramey's Godfather) with us, and were united to our dear Children again on the 19th. Ye of my family, who may ever chance to read this, boast, proudly boast of being lineally descended from Charlotte Upcher, daughter of the Rev'd Henry Wilson of Kirby Cane, Norfolk, from one whom Virtue, Piety, Fortitude, Goodness and Affection would be proud to call their Child!

Tuesday 12th January, 1813.

Return'd to Sherringham to reside, and, the blessing of God accompanying, me, was gradually restored to sound and vigorous health, and I began to take very great pleasure in Farming.

Planted 500 Spruce Firs on Bunkers Hill, digging holes to receive each plant.

In the Spring also planted a small spot that I call Steward's Cover of Spruce, Beech and poplars.

Yellow-wash'd (stone colour) all Cottages belonging to me and got them glaz'd and made comfortable, being much out of repair.

Cut off two pieces of Land for experimental fields or kitchen gardens, planted eight Apple & Pear trees in the upper experimental, and 2 pear trees, in the nitches, on either side the gate of the farm yard, against the gable ends of the Barns.

Planted a few Beech, and some Birch in the Galleries, behind the old House.

on FRIDAY the 2nd of JULY 1813

Henry Ramey Upcher aetatis 3 laid the first stone of our new house, I laid the second, my dear Wife the third, little Mary the 4th and then little Emma, who fell into the mortar, then my Wife's sister Anne, and then my friend Wilkinson who gave the Ceremony its blessing. The Nurse, Esther, my Wife's Maid, & Towler, my servant, each also contributed a stone to the Foundation.

Tuesday the 5th of July – I took my Master of Arts Degree at Cambridge.

19th of June, Repton and his son John Repton came to Sherringham, when the site of the House was finally set out, and the terrace Garden at the back of the House determin'd on.

I had some Pheasants Eggs sent me by Major Wilson, and Mr Sheppard, and by the latter also some french partridges eggs. These I reared, and was afterwards persuaded to destroy them as being very injurious to pointers and sport. The Pheasants Eggs were rotten.

Observe. The Carriage of Eggs should be by hand, as little shaken as possible — game hens are the best nurses.

I built a Lime-kiln, and a Brick-kiln this year — both prove excellent.

I have found the greatest benefit in my Clerk of the works Mr Harrison, master of the Workhouse, who resides in Sherringham, and has daily watch'd the progress of the foundations early and late.

During the building of the Cellars, there were incessant falls of rain, and when cover'd in and having laid many loads of Earth on them, they most imprudently took away the wooden Arches on which the roofs of the Cellars were built, and the whole gave way, causing considerable delay and confusion. But this I regard rather as a fortunate event as there must otherwise have been some sinking in the House, and this accident has made the workmen more careful. The foundations of the house and upper terrace garden wall were completely finish'd by the middle of November. The building then ceased for the year.

I also built a Dog Kennel for my Grey-hounds, this year.

Plough'd up the heath land between the direction post and Mott's new heath-plantations, and planted it, under the management of Mr Fife of Thetford — a belt twenty-four yards wide which in the Spring I intend widening to 80 yds.

Purchases made in 1813

A Cottage and small garden. A good house with small garden and good Barn with an Acre of Land, — of Mrs Creemer for £300.

Three Cottages in Lower Sherringham of D. Devonshire

£......

Two Cottages of old Thursby, situated in the street opposite to the purchase of Creemer, £180.

A farm of 132 Acres, in the occupation of Mr Barcham, of Mr Wells, Queen St. Norwich, for £3000.

We have given all the poor in Sherringham Blankets who have need of them, and my dear Wife has two sets of Childbed linen which she lends to those that are confined, and the women return them wash'd up at the expiration of the month.

Bought the Public House of Patteson of Norwich for £... with its allotment of Heath Land, a triangular piece immediately opposite the spot intended for our upper Lodge.

I have been so happy (thanks be to God) as to reconcile the domestic feuds and quarrels of two familys, and to persuade the son of the principal farmer in the parish to marry his mistress when I had just despair'd of success. I thank God too, that I have been the humble instrument of getting several poor people to receive the Sacrament.

On the 24th of December — We gave away four sheep and four stone of Beef to the poor of Sherringham — 72 families, 334 lbs of Meat for their Xmas dinner.

25th of Decr. Christmas Day — between 80 & 100 people received the Sacrament at Sherringham Church.

All our servants Wives and families dined in our kitchen

and the Children danced with our Children in the Nursery with Esther and the Nurses, and Bell played to them on the fiddle.

It is incredible how the Game increased this year of every kind, but particularly the Hares and Pheasants. The latter I am indebted for to Lord Orford's Covers, for as he did not feed early in the season, and I did, they almost to a Pheasant have come over to my Covers and now, feeding higher on that account, they remain with me, and are to all intents and purposes as much my pheasants as if I had bred them on the spot.

I was this year Churchwarden of the parish and had all the side windows of the Church made to open, and the Windows all cleaned, and the Church white-wash'd, the pulpit also removed to the left from the right side of the Church & the Church painted.

I was also Surveyor of the parish and had the old parish-house, an eye-sore and disgrace to Sherringham, pull'd down, situated next the Church, by which means the Church now boldly opens to the street and our woods also are made more visible to the traveller.

My dear Wife put several Children to School this year.

Thanks be to the Almighty Lord of all Mercies for his un-common mercies vouchsafed unto me this year, for restoring me to perfect health and happiness, and for bestowing on us another pledge of our Love, our dear little infant —

Abbot Upcher born the 25th of September, 1813

Planted a belt 30 yards wide — from the direction post on the Holt Road to Bodham in all 3 acres & ......by Fife of Thetford — the middle of November, he agreeing to put 3,600 plants in each acre, and to warrant them good for 4 years, replacing such as may die, for £10 per annum. But this I already repent, finding I can plant much better and cheaper myself. I never repented any step more, but I was induc'd to do it by my friend Mott who had employ'd him to a very considerable extent.

Sheringham Hall, engraved from a drawing by J. S. Cotman

1814

January — the hardest severest winter known in England for many years — roads completely impassable at times, both to Holt, Cromer & Aylsham.

We gave away two hundred and forty seven bushells of Coals to the poor of Sherringham this month.

And my dear Wife instituted and compleated entirely herself, without any assistance whatever derived from me, the Female Friendly Society at Sherringham, to which I have the happiness of contributing five Guineas annually — before the expiration of the month she had 79 members, but one has already paid the debt of nature.

O 'God' look down with pity on this Society of Poor Friends and prosper them, and bless her O Lord who instituted it.

Latter part of this month commenc'd pruning in the approach thro' the Great Wood.

The Hares distress me beyond measure in barking the Hollies, particularly in Kirby Wood — tho' 3 loads of Swedish Turnips have been carried there this month.

In Kirby Wood had a quadruple Row of Oak Trees next the sea taken up by the Roots, and the ground double trench'd for fresh planting, the old oaks mostly rotten and mere poles, also several men in the Wood double trenching amongst the trees where a sufficient interval allow'd it, in order to sow furze & broom seed & plant box, holly, privet, black & white thorn for under cover, the wood at present being almost entirely bare.

The Snow remain'd deep on the ground till the Middle of March, but the 1st week in February there was a most rapid thaw, and in the 2nd we Coursed at Swaffham. My blue bitch Platoff bore away the Silver Couples in capital style, and out of twenty-three matches that my dogs ran, only five were decided against them.

The latter end of March I began planting under my own auspices and connected the Belt planted by Fife with the great wood according to the directions for the Approach given by Repton. I also planted nine thorns of different kind in groups of three to the right of the approach, and several Sycamores and Beech in the Hedge Rows near, also a belt of Spruce Firs with a few Oak to the left of the great wood as you enter, and also spruce & silver firs to the right to darken the Wood, and exclude the view of the Temple in passing, in order that the Kelling Burst and Walter Scott (the signal station) may appear with greater effect. I also planted a thornery which we call Hawthornden, Laburnums, thorns, Acacias and Mountain Ash, also a great many spruce firs under the Rookery, and on Bluff Point, Beech, Sycamore and Mountain Ash. Behind Ashford's Farm I also planted a

Spruce Fir Belt with Mountain Ash, Larch and Oak in front. The latter end of April I had above an hundred very large hollies brought with balls of earth attach'd, to the Salvator Wood profusely watering them, and on the Victoria hill also planted many spruce and Mountain Ash. But I soon began to suffer from hares. I therefore order'd snares to be set — in less than a fortnight we destroyed 59 hares.

I also made a small plantation to the left of our present house of spruce and silver firs & larch to plant out the Wall, and mountain Ash, Sweet Chestnut, Beech & Sycamore, Lilacs and Thorns with a gravel terrace to walk on.

> 'O'er the glad waters of the dark blue Sea
> Our thoughts as boundless, and our souls as free,
> Far as the Breeze can bear the Billows foam,
> Survey our Empire and behold our Home!'

I also planted a few Beech, Laburnums & thorns with a hope of their hereafter excluding the view of the Roof of our Offices behind the new house.

Major Wilson gave me six hens and one Cock Pheasant which I turned out in March.

Finish'd sowing furze seed in Kirby Wood — May.

On the 5th the body of a Captain of a Merchant Vessel was cast on our Beach. From the report I received of it the body must have been very long afloat.

May — planted potatoes in all my new plantations and ploughed up Patteson's triangular piece and six more yards against Fife's Belt to be sown with potatoes.

23rd. Signed Ashford's Lease — Extent of his Farm 326a. 1r. 29p., the Rent £423. 6. 6.

When Ashford agreed to take this farm corn averaged (Wheat) from 50 Shills. to 60 per coombe. Before he signed it, Peace descended from Heaven and again bless'd the World and Wheat fell to 28 Shills. & 30 per Coombe. Under these circumstances Ashford began to hesitate and express doubts, but on the arrival of his Father they both signed it without any deduction of Rent being made but an agreement on my part to build him a small barn in Upper Deadman's field. I suffered considerable anxiety previous to his signing, for I much feared he would throw up the Farm alltogether. He is to lay on 22 load an acre of Marle on the Farm.

My own Heath Farm -- began paring and burning Scratby Field, and hope to add considerably to the value of my Estate by converting a great deal of the Heath into arable land.

June 1st — Bought of Mott ...... of Heath land intervening Lord Orford and myself. The value of this Land in a sporting point of view is incalculable, and I should think worth at least four times more than I gave for it which was £1250, viz. under £20 per Acre. Mott had paid Fife £110 for planting ...... acres of it, which sum was included in the purchase. For obtaining it at this moderate sum I am indebted to my Wife's calm prudence and reason, for Mott at first ask'd me £1800 for it, which upon my mentioning to Dugmore who had look'd at it for me, he advis'd me by no means to think of giving. Yet still I was more than half tempted to do it, for I much feared that should I not accede to Mott's offer he might repent having ever made it, but my Counsellor Wife begg'd of me to persist, which I at length reluctantly agreed to, and after an interval of about 2 months from the first offer I obtain'd it £550 cheaper than at the first offer.

Some part of this land I shall be able to bring into cultivation.

January 20th. Winter commenc'd with a vast fall of snow, but did not continue many weeks.

Built the Heath Lodge, the residence of my Gamekeeper, Simon Leeder.

Added considerably to the Heath Barn, and built a Bullock shed for my working Devon Oxen.

Repair'd Ashford's Farm Buildings, built new pig sties, calve houses, Dairy & Wash house.

Built a new Granary and Cart Lodge for myself.

Repaired Clarke's house putting an entire new Roof to it.

Imported 60 Chaldron of Coals at £1. 5. 6. per Chaldron, duty 6s. per Chaldn. Coals then selling at 48 shills. per Chal. at the merchants.

Commenced building my Kitchen Garden of which Henry laid the first stone. 28th March.

Agreed to give Fife back his plants in the Heath belt, and he to give me the money I had advanced, a source of great joy to me. I then replough'd it with a four-horse plough, harrow'd it well and replanted it with the best plants I could procure in the Neighbourhood, and I may with truth say it is the admiration of the Traveller who is fond of planting.

Made the Road through the Woods, the Upper Approach, and finish'd and planted the Terrace. I consider this part of the Approach (the Terrace) the greatest possible Masterpiece of Repton's Art in Landscape Gardening. Indeed I thought it impossible at first to make this Road, but the facility with which we executed it is astonishing.

Built the Laundry, the Lower Lodge, a very great convenience and comfort to us.

Studded several hundreds of beautiful Ash plants about the Woods, particularly in the Rookery, and many in the hedge rows of the Cromer Road.

On the 17th of March the Agricultural Meeting took place at Norwich, where we found the Populace were extremely incensed against Mr Coke, he being the great promoter of the Alteration in the Corn Laws, viz. "that no foreign Wheat should be imported into this Country while ours should be under 80s. the Quarter" — an Act which, had it not been pass'd, the Agriculture of England must have perish'd. On coming down the Castle hill, after judging the prizes, where the Mob were in great Numbers, we rallied round Mr Coke, and sustained a shower of brickbats and stones, and it seems to me most providential that some of us were not severely hurt. We got to the Angel Inn, the Mob increas'd to thousands, and after a very long delay Mr Coke in a most fortunate way made his escape on horseback out of the yard the back way with four friends attending of whom Mr Henry Wilson was one. Lord Albemarle was in waiting for him in a post chaise, beyond the Norwich Hospital and they both went to Quiddenham.

5th of April — I went to Holkham myself and saw that beautiful system of wheat Husbandry with the Horse hoe which I cannot sufficiently admire. The wheat is drill'd at 9 Inches, a coomb an acre, and early in the spring horse-hoed, the best possible method of getting clear of weeds. Their fields are like Gardens.

7th of April — Arthur Wilson Upcher was born. I had scarcely return'd home half an hour and sate talking with my dear Wife when she retired, and at 5 minutes past 5 p.m. gave me another Son.

11th of April — sold the great Tythes of Ormesby and Scratby to Edmund Lacon Esqr. M.P. for £17,500, which I consider a very great price. (N.B. Wheat fell after this sale from forty to twenty-three pounds per Load, Barley from £20 to £9 a Load, Oats the same.) This was a property that never afforded me either respectability, pleasure or comfort. I hold that the great object of all landholders should be to concentrate their property as much as possible — this has ever been my object.

13th of April — Laid down the 4 Acres, call'd the Wood, Hill's piece, with sainfoin. The seed for this cost me £12.

Our white bricks for frontage we had from Mr Green's of Wroxham, he delivering them at Aylsham by Water from whence our Wagons brought them.

17th April. Mr Bedford my Clerk of the Works arrived, whose value I could not then know, but whom I have since found to be invaluable.

He advised us, on inspection of our plans, to build our offices this year and to immediately import every necessary article. To this we willingly agreed, & in a short time he sail'd for Hull, and purchased all the Memel Timber [i.e. from Memel in Prussia], Deals, Slate, Plaister of Paris, Lead, Nails etc. The various Cargoes we got safely to our own shore, and by this means acquired our materials at a very diminish'd price to what we could have bought them in the County — I mean in Norfolk. In the article of Memel alone we saved near one shillg & 6d a foot, and the expence of land carriage of twenty-four miles from Norwich. Mr Bedford also agreed for some Oak Wreck at Blakeney and some very valuable timber from a Granary that was then taken down by Mr Brereton. On the inspection of the lime it was found necessary to build another kiln in a different pit, and I rejoice to say that it is consider'd the best lime in the neighbourhood. It has never yet been known to blister in fine plaistering. I regret to say that it was owing to the obstinacy of Harrison that the Kiln was not originally built in the pit it now is, as he knew that it formerly had a lime kiln in it which was much celebrated. For the stone work of our house Mr Bed-

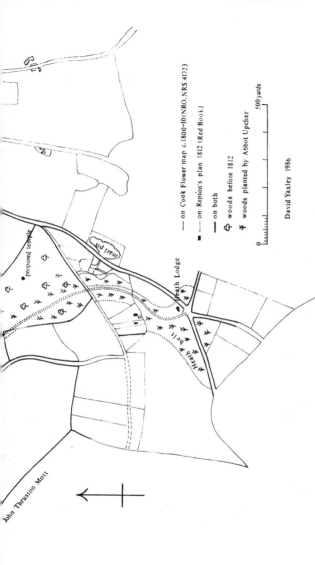

Map of the Sheringham Estate based on Humphrey Repton's sketchmap in the 'Red Book' and a Cook Flower Estate map in the Norfolk Record Office which appears to have been pencilled over in Upcher's own hand.

— on Cook Flower map c.1800-10 (NRO, NRS 4172)
..... on Repton's plan 1812 (Red Book)
■ on both
♧ woods before 1812
⚐ woods planted by Abbot Upcher

David Yaxley 1986

0 ⌊⌊⌊⌊⌊⌊⌊⌊⌊⌊ 500 yards

John Thruston Mott

• proposed temple

marl pit

Heath Lodge

Heath hill

ford agreed with Mr Gray of Aylsham, who went to the Isle of Portland and agreed for the necessary quantity. For the Iron Work Mr Bedford contracted with Mr Dagless of Bodham, for the working of the Lead and painting with Mr … of Cley.

The Foundations, which had now been built near two years, Mr Bd much approv'd & particularly the Cellars which he found all water-logg'd. During the Summer of this year we got nearly all our timber sawn out and every means taken to season it. The Autumn saw our Offices built containing the Brewhouse & Bake house, Scullery, Kitchen, 2 Large Closets for house maids things & billets of wood, Butler's pantry, Store Room, Housekeeper's Room, Servants' Hall, and over these the Nurseries, Harry's Room, the Miss Wilsons' Room, a Spare Room, Lady's Maid Room, Maidservants' Room and the Men's Room. These Offices were infinitely improved by Mr Bd's judicious arrangement. They now serve as workshops for the different Carpenters and Joiners. The rapidity with which our mansion began to rear its head quite astonished its Visitors. But everything was so happily arranged by Mr Bedford whose Eye and Step was every where. The Garden too now began to shew its promising, fruitful South Wall complete — the 3 others were left about breast high. From this Garden at some future period I expect much pleasure. It is a spot to which one may some

22

times steal from the cares of this World and meditate on the mercies of God, and be grateful for them.

At the North East end of it Mr Bedford plann'd the Gardiner's house, a Cottage of great comfort and utility. We had design'd to have built only sheds there for tools, but we were soon convinc'd of the necessity of a Cottage, and the sheds as they rose were converted with little trouble into one.

But to crown the year 1815 we built a School Room, and Charlotte established a School of 40 poor Girls, on the Lancastrian system principally, and praised be Almighty God, it has succeeded far beyond our expectations. Harry and Mary are members of it. I never met with children more fond of reading than they are. Harry this year was perfectly conversant with the Maps of England, Scotland & Ireland and Europe, and knew a great many latin and greek words and this year commenc'd writing.

On the Christmas Day of this year Every family had its dinner from us either of Beef or Mutton.

Charlotte gave an excellent dinner to her Friendly Society in my wheat barn — I mean from the finances of her Club — to half of which she gave petticoats. The names were all mix'd in a basin together & our dear Harry drew them out for prizes or blanks. This was in honor given by Charlotte of my birth Day the 6th of December.

1816

Bank'd up the Primrose wood and enlarged it to the South and studded it with larch, upland Alders, Sycamores & Beech. Made a cover in Sparrow Dale call'd the Hen's Nest, that the Hen pheasants might have a place to breed in undisturbed.

Built a pheasants' house at St. Fillan's spring.

The South Wall of the Garden was planted early this Spring after infinite care bestow'd on the Border. It was dug up a yard deep and paved with shingles at the bottom, over which Marle was spread and beaten down, then various strata of muck, mould, pond mud, etc. fill'd up the whole. The trees were from Mr Mackie's Nursery. The following is the list of them:

Dwafted Bourdini Peach. do. Montaigne do.

1 Standard Old Newington do. 1 do. Noblese do.

1 do. Red Magdalen do. 1 dwafted Galande do.

1 Standd New Hardy White Nectarine. 1 Dft'd Elruge.

1 dwftd Temple do. 1 Standd Temple do. 1 Dft'd Red Roman.

1 Standd Red Roman. 1 Std Newington do.

2 Dftd Moorpark Apricots. 1 Dftd Orange.

1 Standd Green Gage Plum.

1 Dwafted Coe's Seedling.

1 Standard May Duke Cherry

Fig, East Wall.

March 21st. Carted Mould into Garden with 3 teams, and arranged South Plantation for concealing the Garden from Lower Road.

March 20th. Studded 150 Larches behind the Heath Lodge.

The best wheat at this time sells only £27 a Load.

Three London Joiners and three London Carpenters arriv'd early in January to form into Doors, Windows etc. the Timber that had been sawn out in 1815.

March the 18th. The Stone Masons commenc'd putting the portland stone plinth round the basement of the House which gave it a very interesting appearance.

The Well — copy of a letter from Bedford.

"Sir, I am happy to inform you, that the Well makes 1 foot 9 inches water upon an average every day. This morning it had gained two feet 9 inches, which I attribute to the sudden change in the Weather. Taking it at 1 foot 9 inches, the daily supply is 288 Gallons, which is far beyond the consumption of any family." Thos. Bedford

signed Feb. 23d '16

March. The Coal house of the Bowr was built, and the Nursery appendages over them on ......

28th. Various trees, Beech, Ash and Elm put in behind

Ashford's, and 2 Yews close to the Veranda of the Bower.

27th. The beautiful plantation before the outer South Wall made by Jeffery, consisting of some very fine Walnuts, Turkey Oaks, Elms, Planes, Ash, Horse Chestnuts, Larch, Laburnums, Mountain Ash, Yews, American Spruce, Balm of Gilead, was this day planted and afforded me great pleasure, being an elegant means of preventing the Garden being an eye-sore to the Traveller as he approaches our Bower by the Lower Road. N.B. The Plane was never planted in this parish till this day.

During the latter part of March the frost was severely cold.

The Property Tax was this month outvoted by the Opposition in Parliament — a blessing the whole nation sensibly felt, for who did not fear that it might become permanent?

The Malt Tax was given up by the Minister immediately afterwards. (Vansittart)

Leeder's Heath Lodge was this day (the 27th March) studded thick with Beech and Sycamores and behind with beech and Larch and Scotch fir. I found the Silver Firs, that had long been planted there, made but a slight progress there, and could ill resist the extreme cold Winds.

The Junction Belt also to the great Wood from Leeder's was studded with Scotch and spruce.

Some Large Beech in Bluff Point and 4 Horse Chestnuts openly in the Lawn, near the Garden, and 3 near the Flower

26

Garden.

Sycamores were also planted 20 yards apart on the outer part of the Bank leading to the great Wood, from the Heath Lodge.

1st of April 1816 — The main body of the house began to be built.

Easter Sunday, April 14th 1816. Henry Ramey Upcher first went to church at Sheringham.

The severest cold weather this day, the Icicles very long from the sheds of the House.

22nd Ap. Harry and Mary commenc'd writing under Mr Jordan of Gresham.

30th. Commenc'd sowing Rokeby, 16 Acres & ½ a part of our Lawn, 7 sacks per acre hard-land Hay seeds, near 8 lbs of Lucerne just receiv'd from France per acre, 4 lbs of Cow Grass do. & 3 lbs of suckling per Acre.

Imported a cargo 56 Chaldron of Newcastle Coals.

Repton gave us a love-visit in June for 3 days with his son John. They were much satisfied with Bedford's operations and the whole construction of the house.

During the time they staid, they were indefatigable in their exertion to improve our grounds, views from the Bower, and thousand other things.

On the Gravel Pit Close were sown 7 sacks per Acre, hard land hay seeds, 6 lbs per Acre Lucerne, 1 Cowgrass (or perennial Clover) per Acre, Suckling … per Acre, the sandy parts limed and in addition to the other seeds were sown with Cocksfoot Grass which Chester procured me from Gibbs' in London.

2 Bushells of Barley drill'd in both fields at 6 Inches. The average of my drilling barley is always 3 Bushells an acre, but I sow'd but 2 on account of the Grasses that were sown & I trust to flourish in the front of the Bower for many a future year.

May 7th — first sow'd Pacey's perennial Ray grass on six acres of my heath farm with … lbs of Cow grass and … lbs of Suckling.

Rain'd very hard the beginning of this month to the joy of every farmer. There never was a Barley Crop got in or grass seeds sown under happier auspices than during the present month.

May 9th. Howel & his son and Chapman began to throw down the fences in good-acre, that is the particular field in which the Bower stands.

11th. The Thermometer dropp'd to within 5 degrees of the freezing point.

Incessant rain and cold till the 20th with violent gales.

Extreme cold during all May.

ON PLANTING POTATOES

Before you plough your land the last time, put on your manure, then plough it well in, and harrow it down. Then have a plough drawn by one horse, to turn the earth on each side at one time, and which will produce a furrow of six inches width. A man must follow the plough with a tread, who should make his holes about 3 inches apart in which your potatoes should be put by a girl or Boy, who must drop them in, and fill up the hole. The distance between each row of potatoes should be 13 or 14 Inches.

By this way of planting in the bottom of the furrows, early in the spring, the proper time, it always keeps off the frost. They grow precisely in the same manner as Celery. When you hoe your potatoes you will have plenty of Earth to put round them, which will prevent the root from becoming green and appearing above the ground.

The following calculation is worthy notice:

160 roods to an acre
6 bushells to a rood
———
960 bushells to an acre.

Supposing 960 bushells to be sold at 1 sh. a bushel (a very low rate) it would amount to £48 per acre, which again being multiplied by ten will for ten acres of Land produce for potatoes only the surprising sum of £480.

Extract from Thos. Gibbs' 'Expertmental Farmer'.

The following lines whose only merit is the faithful description of our children, were written after a little family dance, when my dear Wife was in a family way and expecting to be confined in June.

THE FAMILY HOP

There was Madam herself, whom the Parish so loves,
And the Sheringham Squire, with his new pair of Gloves,
There was Harry the good, in his fine hussars drest,
And May, with a rose, on her fair snowy breast.
Funny Emma, that some indeed call'd Columbine,
And an Abbot that danc'd in a fantail so fine.
And the Punch, little Arthur, bewail'd with a tear
That his Eleanor* could not till next June appear,
But he found an old partner in Nurse ever kind,
And stirr'd his fat legs, very much to our mind.
So we all in a circle went merrily round,
And the Children seem'd fairies on magical ground,
And shouted aloud — we'll recall this sweet hour,
When we dance, with more strength, in dear
                                    Sheringham's Bower!

*Should our next be a girl we intended calling her Eleanor Augusta — the latter of these was the name of my dear youngest Sister.   A. U.

28th May. The Beams of the chamber floors were fix'd over the Library, Dining Room & my Room & Justice & Bath.

29th of May. 6 minutes before 9 o'clock p.m. our little Augusta was borne. No words can express my feelings of happiness & gratitude to God in finding my Wife quite safely deliver'd and doing so well.

24th of June. Mr Girdlestone baptised our infant daughter, Augusta Elizabeth. The former the name of my dear youngest sister, and the latter of my most revered, most beloved and most honoured Mother.

Septr. 28th '16 — she was vaccinated from the virus sent from the arm of her cousin Louisa Chester, at Denton, which took in both arms.

Lines supposed to be address'd to Lawrence on seeing his ill-drawn portrait of Thomas William Coke Esqr, M.P.

Blush, Lawrence! Blush that e'er thy magic Art
Should fail to move the fond Spectator's heart
When all that Hono'r has so long rever'd,
When all that Virtue has so long endear'd,
Before thee stood, that thou mights't truly give
The Form which Friendship wish'd should ever live,
Live to the Eye as well as Memory dear,
That Ages yet unborn might see it and revere.
But where's the Smile of Him, whose generous Soul,
Whose hand, when Misery pleads, disdain control?
And where the mild, benevolent regard
Ensuring active Industry reward?
In vain, alas, we seek, we strive to trace
The sweet expression of his manly face,
In vain the friendly, candid, noble look
Of grateful Norfolk's pride, her honour'd Coke.
Yet not to Norfolk only had been dear
The form that every Briton must revere,
But like the Sunbeam welcom'd every where,
For every province, were his Image shewn,
Had hail'd and wish'd the Patriot her own.
But go, when universal Joy invites,

And Ceres triumphs in her festal rites,
When flocks are yielding to the Shepperd's care
The spotless treasure of their fleeces rare,
And thou shalt see how Holkham's generous Lord
Receives the meed of praise, his due reward.
Yes, thou shalt hear the zealous praise expres'd
Mid thund'ring shouts of many a distant Guest,
And, long re-echoed, that from Holkham's Hall
The Stream of knowledge flows that fertilizes all!
Then Lawrence, then resume again thy task!
Give to our Eyes the Image that we ask,
Or may some other in a happier hour
Express it with such animated pow'r,
And to our Eyes the wish'd-for Portrait give
E'en as if Art had bid the Canvass live
So true, so faithful that e'er yet 'tis spoke,
Our hearts, our gladden'd hearts, proclaim 'tis Coke!!

These lines I wrote as I was returning from Holkham to Sheringham in my Carrigge where Charlotte and myself had been spending a few most happy days.

I sent them to Miss Coke a few days afterwards.

June 17th. The Walls of the Garden began to rise again. Owing to the judicious plantation of my gardiner Jeffry, I was enabled to have an extra South Wall of Red Brick which unless planted out, I should have consider'd an eye-sore.

July 4th. Had a dish of Pease from the New Garden, which was its first produce.

Septr. 11th. All the Walls of the Garden finished.

During this year there was no summer whatever. Incessant rains during June, July & August, and tremendous gales. On the 1st September there was a perfect hurricane. On our own shore there were three ships wreck'd whose Crews, by the Gallantry of the L. Sheringham men in Captain Manby's Life Boat, were all saved.

Not till the 18th of September did I begin harvest, cutting down my oats.

Incessant rain the latter part of Septr. One day, very fine and windy, was enabled to stack ten Acres and ½ wheat & 8 load of Barley barn'd. Beginning of Octr. incessant rain.

25th. Went over Cranefield's lands with him, of which he had given me the refusal, being about to sell them. Five weeks after he offer'd me 67 acres arable and 30 of Heath, 2 Cottages, for £4,000 which I refused, and then dropp'd to £3,000 which I also refused to give. After another meeting and two letters passing, he agreed to take £2,100 for 59.2.36 of arable land & the Car, and 33 Acres of Heath Land —

purchase agreed to on the 18th Septr. 1816. 8 Acres I refused to buy, being on Mortgage & not his own.

This land we intend calling the Ormesby farm in consequence of being able to advance the money by means of our sale at Ormesby to Lacon.

Septr. The stone plinth around the house very nearly finished.

The slaters busily employ'd on the Roof.

Novr. 6th — finished slating the house.

Visitors to see the Bower this year.

Miss Coke. Mrs Branthwaite. Mrs Anson and 2 Mr Ansons. Doughtys. Mansels. Lord James and Lady Townshend. General Wemyss and family. Septr. 18th Mr Peter and Miss Varlow, Col. and Mrs Wodehouse, Mr and Mrs Wm. Wodehouse & John Wodehouse, the Colonel's eldest son. H. Partridge and Brother D. Lady Suffield and Lady Suffield. 26th Septr. Mr Gregg, Mrs Hibbert & Miss Hibbert. The Gurdons. Tom Mellish, Miss Mellish. Lady Caroline & Lady Tryphina Bathurst.

To Charlotte Wilson

In Tyrant's courts, believe my first
Holds undisputed sway,
But where my whole makes known my first
'Tis Rapture to obey.

My second is a lovely boy,
Fond pledge of dear domestic pleasure.
Unite them and you name my joy,
My hope, and oft in dreams, my treasure.   A.U.

On the delay between the Arrival of the Sparrow and the Fancy
with Lord Wellington's Dispatches

'You peevish old churl!' cried Britannia, inflamed,
To Neptune, while anxious she look'd o'er the Sea,
'My Wellington fought, and you might be ashamed
To keep thus the tidings of Glory from me.'

'Bright Goddess' he answer'd, 'Oh, blame not in thought
Old Neptune who glories in seeing you blest.
By a Sparrow I sent word the Hero had fought
And to Fancy, I thought, I might well leave the Rest!

The Death of Abbot Upcher

Early in 1817 Sheringham Bower was within a few months of completion and the family hoped to move in that summer. But in March the two little Upcher girls, Mary and Emma, walked up to the house with their grandfather and heard him give orders that all work on the new building should cease. Abbot Upcher had been taken seriously ill with a 'violent inflammatory fever'.

At this distance in time it is not easy to diagnose the nature of Abbot Upcher's 'brain fever'. Between 1811 and 1817 his journals and letters refer quite frequently to headaches and restlessness, and occasionally to chest pains. The attack in 1812 described in this journal brought him very low in health and spirits, so much so that, according to letters in Repton's correspondence, he considered selling Sheringham and was only deterred by finding that he could only obtain 30,000 guineas for the estate for which he had given 50,000. He recovered from this bout, however, and it was not until 1817 that he became incurably ill. He was in great danger from March 5th until April 3rd 1817 and then made a partial recovery. The family moved to Brompton, Kent, where Charlotte nursed him devotedly. Sadly it was felt necessary to keep the children away from him to avoid over-excitement. They saw him only occasionally at a distance walking in the garden. The fever returned in January 1819. He suffered a stroke at the end of the month as a result of which he died on February 2nd.

Doctors have suggested two possible diagnoses of Abbot Upcher's disease, tubercular meningitis and subarachnoid haemorrhage. The first could almost certainly have been treated successfully by modern medecine.

The day after Abbot's death Charlotte cut off her hair and some locks of the children's and laid them around the neck of her dead husband. Her mourning was deep and prolonged. She vowed to remain a widow for at least five years and to devote herself unstintingly to her children. She took the estate into her own hands and continued Abbot's interest in the church and parish of Sheringham, planted lime trees in the churchyard and a laurel by Abbot's tomb. As her grief subsided she threw herself into parish activities, her Female Friendly Society, the village school and her free Sunday school for 'hobbledehoys'. In these activities she was aided and supported by Thomas Fowell Buxton and Hannah, his wife, who took the lease of Cromer Hall in 1821 and later moved to Northrepps Hall. Their friendship helped her over the final stages of mourning.

Charlotte never remarried, but her generosity and devotion to good works made her truly the uncrowned queen of Sheringham — 'such a reigning person' Hannah Buxton called her. When, in 1837, her father inherited the title of Lord Berners, she became the Honourable Mrs Charlotte Upcher and was known to the servants as 'The Honourable'. Sheringham Bower or Hall was not completed until 1839 when the newly-married Henry Ramey Upcher moved into the house with his young wife. Charlotte Upcher lived on in the old farm house until her death in 1857.

EDITORIAL NOTE

The original of this journal is written into a leather-bound volume now in the possession of the H. T. S. Upcher Trust. It was clearly intended to be a full record of the building of Sheringham Bower. Sadly only about a quarter of the book was ever used.

Abbot Upcher's spelling has not been changed. His punctuation, which consists largely of a liberal and haphazard sprinkling of dashes, has been amended to conform with modern usage.

I am indebted to the doctors of Fakenham Surgery, and to Mr G. Bolt of Queen Elizabeth's Hospital, King's Lynn, for the medical opinions expressed in the note on the death of Abbot Upcher.   S. Y.

The Upcher Children

Henry Ramey Upcher, born 1810, educated at Harrow and Cambridge, married Caroline Morris in 1838 and lived at Sheringham Bower after his marriage.

Charlotte Mary Upcher, born 1811, married Edmund Charles Buxton, the nephew of Thomas Fowell Buxton. He was a banker and they lived first at Hendon and later at Chigwell, Essex.

Emma Upcher, born 1812, married John Robert Pigott of Doddershall Park in 1835. He became curate of North Marston, then vicar of Hughenden, Bucks., then rural dean. He later obtained the living of Ashwellthorpe and Wreningham and the family lived at Rainthorpe Hall until his death in 1852.

Abbot Upcher, born 1813, educated at Harrow and Cambridge, married Mary Jones Day. He became curate at Flixton then rector of Kirby Cane until his death in 1889.

Arthur Wilson Upcher, born 1815, educated at Harrow and Cambridge and rowed in the first Boat Race in 1836. He was curate to John Pigott at Hughenden for two years, then curate of Upper Sheringham and, after Pigott's death rector of Ashwellthorpe and Wreningham.

Augusta Elizabeth Upcher, born 1816, died of consumption at the age of twenty.

Further information about the Upchers may be found in:
'A History of Sheringham and Beeston Regis'
by A. Campbell Erroll
'The Banville Diaries'
edited by Norma Virgoe and Susan Yaxley